SPLIT THE SEA

Poems by Jacob Plante

www.PoeticaPublishing.com

Cover Art:
"Masks and Eyes"
by Bruce Rolff
ShutterStock.com
Image #1017912640

Published by Poetica Publishing
www.PoeticaPublishing.com

Printed in the United States of America.
ISBN: 978-1-942051-28-2

This book is dedicated
to my parents, David and Deborah,
and to my son Adam.

Table of Contents

Various Poetry

About the Author

Bipolar Poetry

Check the Pulse

It's a little hip if you love me
it's a little hip if you don't
and i'ma break down
like most people won't
it's the way it is will and was
don't ask why just because

impulse is the pulse
that runs through my veins
chemicals flow unevenly
throughout my brain

you hear voices on the phone
I hear voices in my head
i'm more imaginary than
drop dead fred
i've walked so many miles
in so many shoes
i'm sub arctic
seven levels below the blues
strive to stay alive
clarity is so confused
seven times over i've paid my dues
so how do you stop
a train headed for disaster
you know you should slam the breaks
but you crank it up faster

impulse is the pulse
that runs through my veins
chemicals flow unevenly
throughout my brain

i'm searching to be free
from torment inside of me
stretch vast at last
reach up to the sky
i'm a king i'm a martyr
i'm Jesus Christ
don't ask why

impulse is the pulse
that runs through my veins
chemicals flow unevenly
throughout my brain

kick it flip it
stop drop and get with it
let us make no mistake
struggle to be alive most every day
my hearts a mangy cur
a back alley stray
roam for home all alone
it's a shame
that nobody listens when I pray
so i'ma get sick with no delay
ancient meditations
and medieval evil thought
delusions with fragmentation
look what your tax dollars bought
i'm a king i'm a martyr
i'm The Buddha Siddhartha
i'll bring peace to the world
and doom to the wicked
while i'm curled up in the corner
crying in a fetal position

impulse is the pulse
that runs through my veins
chemicals flow unevenly
throughout my brain

Untitled Sickness

ima bout to spit some script
lets make a hit
gettin' wicked sick
from Hamtramck
it happens to be my location
and kickin funky tush rhymes
is just my occupation
being mentally ill torrmented
is just my situation
so here we go on the MD tip
manic depressive
so go get hip with it

I'm manic
and a fanatic
got crazy thoughts
locked up in my attic
my mind races
and I begin to panic
i hear strange voices
and static
my heart drops
from the ceiling to the ground floor
once more
i can't take this illness
i've just had it
my minds wandering
as if it was nomadic

i'm feeling opposites
and extremes
and everything in between
from lunar to solar

why did G-d make me bipolar
i can't handle this roller coaster
next time i take a bath
ima drop in some bubbles and a toaster

don't tell me you understand
that statements just hazy
you'll never ever know
what its like to be this crazy
neurotransmitters not connecting in my brain
its a reaction chain
and i'm going insane
delusional
mentally ill
the thoughts i spill
sometimes overkill
i take too many pills
i've had my fill
can't afford the medical bills
ready to jump out window sills

emotions so anonymous
yet heavier than a hippopotamus
don't ask me
cause i just don't know
i can't write prose
but it goes to show
i can express like a pro
explaining my highs and lows
the way my mood flows
pop that medication
a double dose
paranoia has me walkin' on my toes
three times denial as the cock did crow

my brain is overextended
its about to erupt and blow
so its hi ho hi ho
its off to crazy we go

i'm spendin' all my cheddar
a manic shoppin spree is better
than my bill collection letters
i can't socialize with humanity
i've unbearable social anxiety
try to stay humble with piety
but these delusions of grandeur inside of me
keep leaving me to believe
that i'm a deity
so please leave me
with three bottles of anti-freeze
as I drop to my knees
to gulp it down with a breeze

as i stop
then i drop
with four on the floor
i see angels on a ladder
and i cease to breathe
my heart stops beating
and my soul is free

Underdog

sometimes
i get a thrill
from being mentally ill
its a crime
bipolar in the summertime
but it's so ice cold chill
when i get to lay it down
to those few
that i'm tormented
diseased in the brain
handicapped
and i'm still better than you

my cest pool is deeper
than your clear blue ocean
i got this notion
that even though you're nutritious
my vibe is more delicious
even though i've got delusions
of confusion
my beautiful expressions
leave you superstitious
deep depression
grandeur mania
strange rhyming Albania

my life is so complicated
yet life is so simple for you
yet i'm super educated
i'm smarter than spock
i have a PhD from
the university of hard knocks
you'll never compare to me

and you're in the dark
my struggle you will never know
and you may sometimes win the bronze
but i'll always win the gold

The Way It Is

I'm manic
and a fanatic
got crazy thoughts
locked up in my attic
my mind starts to race
and I begin to panic
i hear strange voices and static

whats going on
this feels like phase one
of an episode that's just begun
i'm not getting any sleep
I'm talking none
this sure ain't fun
if I could escape this
i wouldn't jog i'd run

my sanity is about to collapse
i think i'm having a relapse
mania is the only thing I grasp
i can't handle this
this has gone too far
sanity i truly miss
I've got too many scars
and battle wounds
from manic episodes
i'm sick of padded rooms
spring please come again
i want to be in bloom
instead of certain doom
why'd i ever leave the womb

may the sun shine
upon my face
in due time
i'll be away from this place
i pray again for stability
immediately
followed by mobility

Suffer Journey

When I wake up in the morning
the hardest thing to do
is live
When I wake up in the morning
the hardest thing to do
is go on
one more day
blood no longer flows
through my veins
only pain reigns

I dream
I hope
I laugh
I somber
I mope
I cry
I scream
I die

these eyes see a world
that my mind does not
my hands touch feelings
that my heart has not
real
what is real
let it be and keep it
fantasies are born from reality
realities are born from mere fantasies

tick tock tick tock
arms on the clock
tiny sounds
intensified by silence

drive me to a place
where I already exist
crazy

your words that you swallow
are hollow
when you begin to speak
I begin to tune out
empty comfort
just understand that you don't understand

the moon controls the tides
there is no moon for my emotions
death is a mistress
the inhale of every breath
is one more moment of distress

the easiest thing when I walk through the day
is to know that I don't know
I don't know much
about much
this is my only strength

certitude
confidence
fortitude
determination
backbone
tenacity
foreign language to my spirit

anxiety
bewilderment
skepticism

confusion
ambivalence
indecision
back of my hand

this feeling is ineffable
words and poems
can't begin to describe
what I try to describe
with words and poems
describing the undescribed

triangle
square
circle
trapezoid
rhombus
hexagon
what is my shape

The hardest thing when I go to bed at night
is to fall sleep
The hardest thing to do when I go to bed at night
is to get my mind to be quiet
it races
it paces
driving me crazy
take me away from these places
it's keeping me up
my central system
is making me nervous
the body needs rest
and I need dreams
to take me away from this world

Once Again up to That Breech

how could this be,
this happened to me,
i'm constantly,
being chopped down like a tree,
i just don't foresee,
mania leaving me be,
i want to be free,
of this crazy disease,
will G-d save me,
if I beg Him please,
i'm sick of suffering,
this better get better to a degree,
finer with time like cheddar cheese,

i'm about to explode,
i can't handle another episode,
why must i travel this road,
my heart is about to corrode,
i can't tell the point of overload,

please G-d will you save,
i'm sick of dreamin' of my grave,
this road i'm on please do pave,
take me off this manic tidal wave,
i do mean to rant and rave,
this is not fair,
do you really care,
if so why did you put me here,

we've been through this before,
why's it gotta happen once more,
must be something better in store,
my spirit is broken and sore,

i can't take it anymore,
lift me like a bird and help me soar,
you don't have to knock,
i'll unlock the door,
just make a deposit,
cause i'm mentally poor,
and i'm sick to the core,
filling up with rage,
like a wild boar,
i need you to guide me through,
please don't ignore,
that's how you did me before,

this is too much to bare,
living day to day in fear,
of delusions so grand,
please hold my hand,
and guide me to the promise land.

Mental to the Izzle

I'm mentally ill,
the rhymes i spill,
sometimes overkill,
i take too many pills,
can't afford the medical bills,
i've had my fill,
ready to jump out window sills,

I know sometimes i get a little insane,
tryin to keep my head in the game,
while being manic-depressive,
passive-aggressive,

Is life too long,
or is it too short,
gotta keep my heart strong,
and relax with some port,

My brain is messed up,
I'll never get it back,
out of luck,
I'm way beyond wack,

delusions so grand,
you wouldn't understand,
it hurts so bad,
that you think its just happys and sads,

but its so much more,
its a daily war,
sometimes i get washed ashore,

if only you truly knew,
the things i go through,
no rhymes that i spew,
can ever explain,
whats happenin in my membrane,
when i'm going insane,
i'm in overdrive in the fast lane,
but I try to find piece,
like a paper crane,
Ok to heck with it here i go,
i'm gonna let you in the know,
i've claimed to be G-d,
i've claimed to be Christ,
I once thought I was Bob Barker,
from the Price is Right,
I once thought I was a general,
of a heavenly army,
screaming at traffic cause,
i thought they couldn't harm me,
i shouted at the cops,
and said who do you think you are the police,
so that officer,
pulled out and pointed his piece,
aimed right at my head,
i thought for sure i was dead,
i said i shall fear no man but the lord,
right then the officers knew,
i was out of my gord,
which i am and was,
and these facts i wont mince,
praise the G-d of Israel,
that they called an ambulance,
sent to the hospital,
for months at a time,
not just once but numerous times,

i'm running out of rhymes,
you may hear silence,
but my brain hears chimes,
also chants and rants,
and strange ideas people supplant,
but away with the world,
whose to say i can't,
overcome these things,
and function like a man,
i know i can,
thats my master plan,
one day at a time is the program,

I can do it cause i got the will,
even though i'm mentally ill,
just like my main man,
Winston Churchill.

If You Know What I Mean

i'm the opposite
of dull
my brain fell out of
my skull
cock and bull
is full
with emptiness
insane
went my membrane
the number 13 train
with all the ball
and chain gang
you know how that hammer
swings
ring a ding ding
ain't no thing
as the birds sing
because i clipped
there wings
where's waldo
you never know
what life brings
these crazy things
disguised blessings
turtle dove
from above
thin line is mine
between hate and love

What it Do

now ima drop science
like i was notorious
the magma that i flow
is just so glorious

the love you give
equals the love you make
you gotta jump outta the boat
to walk on the lake

and when you're spendin riches
from that phat gucci purse
remember that there ain't
a luggage rack on that hearse

from the life i've lived
and what i've seen
nothing from nothing leaves nothing

i'm confirmed a buck private
in this crazy war
my agape flows from the heart
cause that's what its for

i found a rose bush
from around the way
so i stopped and took a whiff
without delay
and i be in awe of the great spirit every day
for bestowing to us the gift to pray

now some get manic
and some get depressed
some give up all hope
and that creates a mess
if you don't study hard
you might flunk the test

tweedle dee and tweedle dum
three little birds on my doorstep
and rum pum pum pum

i got what it takes
to make myself ill
i always get the shakes
come time to pop that pill
you take it away
and i don't want anymore
one day i'm gonna lose the war

i stare at the sky
and ask God why this
he said it's not for me to question
and then he blew me a kiss

so this is life
i was handed this lot
i'll struggle through the strife
and rota-till my own plot
constant i love me - i love me not
working hard to re-connect all the dots

these delusions are wrong
but they feel so right
such an overload of mania
i can't sleep at night

voices of people not in the room
visions so psychedelic
did i just eat sum magic mushrooms

committed to the ward
over and over again
each time its so hard
i wish this cycle would end

put me on the clothes line
hang me out to dry
all the stigma in the world
brings me to my knees and i cry

but there's a greyhound coming through
i would take it if i could
and i would not lie to you
because sunday morning soon will come

when the things will be much easier to say
upon the microphone like a poetry slam
and ima jump outta that boat
like the sea was dry land
the freshest poet ain't nothing but a man

to abba belongs my heart my soul my mind
this curse is somehow a blessing and one of a kind

Jewish Poetry

Split the Sea

born into this
concrete jungle
disarray
everyday with
western society
overbearing with Christmas

I've got this primal
tribal
tendencies inside of me
secular Jew
isolation frustration
spiritual deflation
separation from my nation

fast cars and bars
alcohol is king of all
i'm rollin' with
thugs with drugs
sluts with butts
hippies with mushrooms
jokesters and cokesters
funky junkies

i need escape
there is no meaning in these ways
split the sea and i'll flee

i look to the sky
where my help come from
inflate my
soul its
crying out to be nurtured

hashem hashem
give me water for
i am thirsty
dehydrated
i cry for your mercy
i want torah
give me your torah of love
and i will keep it
i packed for the yeshiva
while dreaming in hebrew
studying feverishly

i drank from the wellsprings
with my chosen people
the children of Israel
we got life
the middle road called
truth
torah
opens up my brain and puts
knowledge of G-d inside

this oasis i've been searching for
hashem allowed me to drink some more

i've existed
as two
different Jews
during this human timeline
one of these Jews must flea
the other
there's already a split in the sea
my brother
i've severed my being
to split the tides of darkness
from this see of light

shalom means hello
i speak shalom to
this Jew
whom seeks
righteousness

shalom means goodbye
i spoke shalom to
that Jew
whom sought
wickedness

shalom means peace
and wholeness
shalom echoes
throughout
my soul

they call me
baal teshuva
or to put it in English
master of return

my heart is in flames like a
lion roaring
blazing eternal inferno
burning for hashem
to his torah i return
closer and closer
i draw to you
this thirst is unquenchable
yet you fill my soul
and my cup it overfloweth

hear O' Israel
hashem is our G-d
hashem is One

goodbye to
the darkness it
is gone
it would only bring me down
it would make life too complex
when it's so compound
i'm elevating my soul
i'm purifying my renown
i'm drowning in his love
raise me up
i will be light
shining on

B'nai Yisrael

Sh'ma Yisrael
Hear O' Israel
for over sixty years
you have had Ha Atzmaut
Independence
in another sixty years
will you still be there
for my grandchildren to make aliyah
for Jews to unite behind a homeland
will you have yourself in an orderly state
three thousand years
with no place to be
until this last century
in the next sixty will you still be
the land of milk and honey
will things have changed
will your name be Palestine
will your book be the Koran
will you flourish with evangelist
will Jesus of Nazareth be your anointed one
will we still be able to call you Zion

King David said it like
Hodo al eretz v'shamayim
vayarem keren l'amo
t'hilah l'khol khasidav
liv'nei Yisrael am k'rovo

Sh'ma Yerushaleim
Hear O Jerusalem
Your name means city of peace
have you lived up to your name
there is finally
a united Jerusalem

under Jewish rule
but will a conqueror
with plans to conquer and divide
leave you once again divided
will you still have walls
or when my grandchildren
pilgrimage to your limits

will you be but a mere
archeological excavation site
will they only read about
the capital of their people's
land in school text books
you are the home of the Knesset
and we have questions
put two of us in a room
and you will get three opinions
so there are many questions
and Jerusalem
we need to know
will we still be able to call you Zion

The Prophet Elijah said it like
oseh shalom bim'romav
hu ya'aseh shalom aleinu
v'al kol Yisrael v'imru

Funky Jew Style

wearin' my tzitzit
while i beat heat
on this concrete street
strings so neat neat
feelin' so sweet sweet
hummin' along
with the song
of birds as they tweet tweet
the length
of my spiritual strength
will not deplete
this is oh so sweet sweet
wearin' my tzitzit

Funky Junky

put it in that spoon
gazing at that moon
hold that silver
over that lighter flame
mad game insane
derail this train
lift up load up
that syringe
time to binge
slip that needle
into my skin
inject my veins
with your torah
of love
don't hesitate
shoot it straight
to my heart
and brain
make it rain
pour
thunder
from above
once a week
on shabbat grant
me that fix
through six days
i do my kicks
until that next fix
i crave that double flame
of those candle wicks

Chavatah Gadol

ancient meditations
mystic vibrations
forget what you know
so far
thunder
as the shofar blows

expanding
while compounding
the sound of sounding
creation realization
astounding
profounding

limitless limit capacity
spaceless space
the audacity
of mind blowing tenacity
so far the shofar
behaves like radio-waves
expanding through outer-space
going oh so far
further than the furthest star

Hollow Cost

my babies my babies
barbed wire and iron
divide us
our loving bond
unites us
if we are to die
let us burn flesh to bone
in an incinerator together
they're taking
my two sons
my babies my babies
are going on a different train
to a different concentration camp
my boys aren't even Bar Mitzvah
they needed me to live
they will need me to die
don't let my babies die alone
they need their mother
my babies my babies
I scream and I cry
I shout my babies my babies
as the butt of a Nazi
riffle is smashed into my jaw

Jewish Haiku

Sh'ma Yisrael
we are roots of the same tree
supporting To Life

Jewish Limerick

There once was a Jew from New York
who disguised himself as a dork
he went incognito to a deli
to stuff his fat belly
full of dairy and pork

Jewish Meditation Box

i got this tefillin
body healin'
mind feelin'
binding my nefesh
to torah
before the day's dealin'

roll
with this scroll
bound upon my arm
my king my father
my refuge from harm

wraps
with these straps
kosher leather
on tap

roll
with this scroll
bound between my eyes
realize
with all your modekha
lifted up through the sky

get phat
spit that
mystical voodoo
in a spiritual hue
you know how we do
with that ancient hebrew

sh'ma yisrael
hashem elokeinu
hashem ekhad

meditation infused
forward on
to pay my dues
every day
as i walk through these days

stay away dismay stray from the daze
negativity at bay
navigation of maze

twilight unto the heights
compound this sound
rise up through it all
stumble and fall
get up get get down

shining sunlight with its rays
meditation induced
to guide my pathways
give me walk while i praise

tefillin
body healin'
mind fealin'
tribal jewish chillin'

Kike

i've been called
Kike
before
directly to my face
it was a dagger
in the eye

immediately after
i was told by
that belligerent drunk
shmuck
that the
Jews have ruined the world
since the dawn of time
but it was
okay
because six million
of them gave their
lives
as an apology

what do you
say to this
silence
is the only way

pain
anger
bottled up
aftermath
i wish i could
stab this man
in the eye

but that would
make me
no better
than him

i cry on
my G-d's
shoulder
and ask him
why must
we be hated

Bashert

i'ma flow silly
keepin' it kosha' dilly
crazy young jew
in the motor city
so whattaya do
when its time for shidduch
and your town's situation
is an elderly population

keep your head up trod on
it's called a shadchan
to help in this nitty gritty
searchin' the world
for a curly haired girl
whom mostly reside in New York City

modest and honest
alarming and charming
stunning and funny
debonair
checklist this questionnaire
curly black hair
my only question about this wife
is when does she arrive

Kosher Pickles

kosher kosher
these pickles
are kosher
according to torah
but can i eat
them

yes
i can i see a
hekhsher
they are kosher
rabbinicaly

wait
this hekhsher
its certification
is done by
a reform rabbi
what are his standards
i must follow
kashrut

i must throw this
jar of pickles
into the
trash
while impoverished
Jews in
Israel hunger
for kosher pickles

Left to Right

snap crackle pop
of the sizzle
as we drizzle
through this life
rasha in my left
tzadek in my right
get a handle
on this candle
it can't fizzle all night
drawn from the water
flame creates light
sunny
milk and honey
lead by your hand
to the land
of honest promise
death is a bittersweet
end of the candle wick
gettin' sick
from the thought of
my own extinguished flame
redirect my aim
to proclaim your name
as my candle becomes lame
and shines no more
help me own it
in that last moment
as my spark
becomes dark
and i scream out cries
through the sky
hashem hashem
hashem why this

as you whisper to
my heart that this
is not for me to
question as you
blow me a kiss

Progressive Flow

pass me the laser beam
i'ma bout to
wipe out the wicked and clean
it's out of control
this flow

wake up in the mornin'
and it's hard to live
what else can i give
i would be up
for doggystyle
with a ho
whadaya know
sinnin' on the down low
with no
where to go
snortin' kosher blow

make that money i don't know
these shiksa ho's
tear out your heart
and soul
dispense it on the floor
goyim dime store whore

you give all you can
still they want more-ah
it's scary
to mix that meat
with that dairy
make ya' stray away
from the torah
to sodom and gomorrah

devise
and revise
the master plan
stan the man

crossroads
got ya' turnin'
your head
the unpaved
gravel road to life
or the smooth concrete
highway of the dead

Sunset

sweet sunset
so i can forget
the rest of the week
with these hebrew
words that we speak
oh dearest sunset
sweeter than
romeo and juliet
shakespearean hebrew
arrows that we sling
with these praises we sing
sunset
let us not forget
ourselves
as we use these
hebrew siddurs
off the shelf
oh sweetest sunset
shall i compare thy love
to romio and juliet

The New Style

i'm a crazy jew
who fell
rock bottom
i fell seven times
fell in love with you
you big jew
in the sky
apple pie
goes my eye
thank you mam'
and ooh my my
love you as i lye
love you as i sit
love you as i die
get hip to it
stop drop
and kick it
you erase my wicked
its not even a must
but you
make me righteous
with your torah
of mercy and love
from above
my jewish turtle dove
i'm hooked on you
i can't get enough

Vengeance

let's kick it
i bring doom
to the wicked
with words that i
slay
with a double edged
sword
stay away
scripture readin'
leavin' you bleadin'
i'm compounding your conscious
like physics
breathin'
syllables of fire
mystic envisions
that deconstruct
your darkest provisions
i got spiritual grammar
that swings wrath filled glory
crushing like a doom filled hammer
in this never
ending story
engulfing like the sun
with eternal glory
my G-d is one
end of story

Various Poetry

Acoustic

i string you along
and as you pull on
my strings
i work wonders
and do beautiful things
with your soul

as i'm rested on your knee
i devise
as you create surprise
i perform spiritual surgery

harmony does sooth
through rhythm i do prove
to lose you
in this moment
like a tourist lost in tokyo
you own it
as the melody does flow
eyes to the sky
no form shape or size
as your spirit cries
on my shoulder
i'm your rock your boulder

invisible vibrations
rhythmic calculations
volcanic eruptions
time and space deconstruction

magic from afar
guitar
power bar
open chord

thank the L-rd
hammer on
bend til' dawn
slide
with pride
pentatonic scale
will not fail

held up with that
hippy strap
while you drum tap
drop D tuning
i'm honey mooning

i have six wondrous
strings
for you to pull
as i string you along
and i do soulful things
with your beauty

Auction Block

loud yelling
and chatter
in words i
don't understand
my sisters are
next to me
my aunt
my mother
i her daughter
chatter chatter
as we stand in
front of this crowd
shackled in chains
still alive from
the passage over
the strange
hammer pounds again
men stop chattering
my sister is manhandled and
yelled at and whipped
she is the third to
go
the light skinned ones
are gone
only us dark ones remain
men chatter
in a language we don't
know
there is no escape
from this chatter

Awake & Broken

Crack Smash Shatter
goes the sound of my dreams
now nothing else matters
let me paint the scene
life has its twists and turns
as I plot and scheme
now my heart must un-yearn
from something I will never be
a Los Angeles actor hot shot
fast cars and cash money is what I got
cruising the sunset strip
what are you going to do next
I'm going to Disneyland
making the most of the left coast
bridging the gaps with the unspoken
only to awake to a life that's broken

Crack Smash Shatter
goes the sound of my dreams
what's more to know
Crack Smash Shatter
goes the sound of plan B
as I plot and scheme
a New York City actor hot shot
pastrami on rye at Carnegie deli
washing it down with a Snapple
living life large in the big apple
bridging the gaps with the unspoken
only to awake to a life that's broken

Crack Smash Shatter
goes the sound of my dreams
the nemesis of perfection
the necessary redirection
that lead to a shattered plan C
as I plot and scheme
a Chicago actor hot shot
Second City star
known from the south side
all the way up to Evanston
get up turn around and get down
deep dish clogging my veins
while I'm making it rain
like Al Capone in Chi-town
bridging the gaps with the unspoken
only to awake to a life that's broken

Crack Smash Shatter
goes the sound of my fears
disappointment is too familiar
after all these years
just split the sea and I'll flee
as I exodus towards a plan D
the time is ripe to plot and scheme
I won't leave a single word unspoken
I'm not going to settle for a life that's broken

Silly Poem

Stop I'm fantastic
I don't mean to get spastic
or to get drastic
its just that my arms
are made out of plastic
I eat lucky charms
with a cup of almond milk
snap diggity smooth as silk
I rhyme so nice
like Vanilla Ice
I don't like lice
I study torah
morning noon and night
so I can shine my light
back to square one
when the fun did begun
Stop I'm fantastic
I don't mean to be drastic
or to get spastic
but it's just that my legs
are made out of plastic
I eat fake eggs
they're called egg beaters
I have an uncle Peter
I used to date
this girl named Nora
now all I do
is study torah
it's good for my brain
I have a son named Adam
he watches Thomas the train
I don't like the rain
or any neck pain

when I need to stay sane
I eat bagels that are plain
did I mention that
I like torah
and I light the menorah
sniggity do sniggity snap
talk to my butt
he's the only one that gives a crap
I'm more serious than
flat Stanley
macho manly
Stop I'm fantastic
I don't mean to get spastic
or to get drastic
it's just that my belly
is made out of plastic
I'll eat at a deli
pastrami on rye
why'd they cancel bill nye
the science guy
that show was so fly
every night I cry
myself to sleep
I'm so lonely
this just cut deep
ouch that hurts
I don't rent cars from hertz
I hate my life
there's nothing funny
about that
I wear a little black hat

High & Low

Years from now
will the generations know
how high on my body
I wear my pants
seriously, it's 1940
will my descendants understand
what it's like in 1940
because I wear my pants really high
in the nineteen 60s 70s 80s 90s
and in the 2000s
people will wear their pants
at their hips
or even lower when
in all actuality
the natural waist line
is right above one's belly button
I'm thinking of the future pant line
and realizing that
Oh My God
I am wearing my pants so high
in the 1940s
maybe our pants have to
be made by the tailor
to be longer than yours
because we wear them so high
we wear our pants high
really high
really really high
really really really high
really mother effing high
you shoot from the hip
we shoot from the natural waist
wait just one darn tootin' minute

maybe we don't wear our pants high at all
you just wear your pants low
what is the state of the union that
pants have come to being worn so low
really low
really really low
really really really low
really mother effing low
so low that people
can see your dupa
you wear your pants really low
like we think you have a job as a plumber
that kind of really low

Ten Years in the Making

sweat
blood
tears
four
years
of schooling
each one a
lap around the
track
with many extra
victory laps
you slaved
like you
were under
the yoke of
Pharaoh
you juggled
jobs
family
illness
friends
classes
exams
as if you were
Barnum & Bailey
each lap
harder than
the next
inspiration
perspiration
obligation
frustration
regroup
from regrouping

struggle
we shall overcome
rise above
sprint that
final lap
yellow tape
Graduation
move that tassel
you've earned it

The League of Friends

I remember back in the day
having many best friends
and we used to say
that when we grew older
we would never part ways
not now or not ever
that we would be best friends
right now and forever
because friendship never ends
but times change and people move on
night turns into day
and dusk becomes dawn
because there's friends of the past
and friends that last
some friends come and go
and some quite fast
I remember every single friend
growing up in my youth
maybe someday
I'll say
that I remember you
maybe later in life we'll
cross paths out of the blue
saying to each other
hey I remember when
we shared that moment
way back then
we'll laugh and smile
maybe even grab a beer
only to forget each other
later on that same year
but I remember buddies

pals and chums
and pleasantries
as they would go and come
when I think back on the past
I have so many memories
given by my friends
and I carry them with me
as I walk through life
they may bring me good cheer
in times of strife
but as I sit and I ponder
a friend and their memory
I have to sit and wonder
do they remember me

Trio Freestyle

he's the biggest little bird
on cardinal parkway
make way
he's got street cred
in his chuck taylor shoes
as he tweets those high and low blues

his neighbor woodrow
the dopest woodpecker
he steps outside to jam
so swell
with his machine gun tap
like a bat out of hell

now the stage is set
it's all good in the hood
to come and snuff the
rooster
crowing only like peter
pan could

tweet snap cockle-do rat a tat tat
get phat
ain't nothin' but a chicken wing ding
to skat like that

Sappho in D Minor

The glow and beauty of the stars
the staunch aroma
of the pasture
the sweet smell of
your lustful beauty
your nectar
delicious
your flower is in bloom
its pedals
bring forth tantalizing flavors
to be devoured by love

The Feathered Three

I awoke to the sun blazing through my curtain
a grin suddenly hit my chin
out on the stoop were birds of three
how could I ever have been certain
that these birds would bring joy to me
I stepped outside and took a seat
then they started flowing to this wicked beat

sayin' put all your cares away
carpe diem seize the day
everything is gonna be okay
we say what we mean and mean what we say

I awoke to the sun blazing through my curtain
a grin suddenly hit my chin
out on the stoop were birds of three
how could I ever have been certain
that these birds would bring joy to me
I stepped outside and took a seat
then they started flowing to this wicked beat

sayin' put all your cares away
carpe diem seize the day
everything is gonna be okay
we say what we mean and mean what we say

I awoke to the sun blazing through my curtain
a grin suddenly hit my chin
out on the stoop were birds of three
how could I ever have been certain
that these birds would bring joy to me
I stepped outside and took a seat
then they started flowing to this wicked beat

sayin' put all your cares away
carpe diem seize the day
everything is gonna be okay
we say what we mean and mean what we say

sayin' put all your cares away
carpe diem seize the day
everything is gonna be okay
we say what we mean and mean what we say

The Seven Seas of Rhyme

i got pirate treasure
they call it booty
i found it down under
with this ausie cutie

this girls got curls
from around the way
they say
it's a pleasure
she gives good treasure

sailin' the seas of rhyme
like it was a crime
cause i'm down for mine
in the easy summertime

silly kosha' dilly
as we make some more milly
my name is beverly
and i'm a hillbilly

sailin' the seas of rhyme
like it was a crime
cause i'm down for mine
in the easy summertime

squash the competition
with repetition
like your grandma's garden
beg your pardon
haven't you heard
three and a third
is the word

and i'm an awkward nerd
must i repeat
they call me repeat pete

sailin' the seas of rhyme
like it was a crime
cause i'm down for mine
in the easy summertime

Untitled Sorrow

i wish that i could rap like MCA,
then i'd be the hippest DJ,
from around the way,
and make all the girlies say,
that i can get down,
from the underground,
with that beastie sound,
from that New York town,
kickin' Root Down,
yellin' all around,
he almost spits like MCA,
who was the greatest DJ,
known to date,
who could rock the stage,
from New York to LA,

i wish i coulda met him,
he rhymed above the rim,
in the streets and gym,
influence of my youth,
that's G-d's honest truth,
made such an impact,
as i sit to pray,
if there only was a way,
we could bring you back,
you made this world so grand,
royal were you man,
i want to shake his hand,
tell him what his music did for me,
he and the beastie three,
Ebidnago Meshakh Shadrakh,
MCA Ad Rock and Mike D,

the world will never be the same,
now that your gone,
in our hearts you live on,
your memory keeps us going strong,
as we trod on,
blessed with your presence,
forty-seven years long,
better than eight days of presents,
you made earth a better place,
for this young yid,
and for the human race,
with all that you did,
inspiration as we rise and fall,
you gave it your all,
what more could you giva,
met never did we,
but you were family to me,
when you passed i sat shiva...

About the Author

Jacob Plante was born and raised in Midland Michigan and graduated from Herbert Henry Dow High School. He then moved to the Detroit area to start a career in Standup Comedy. He later got involved with improv, he studied at The Second City, and was an ensemble member of the troupe Big Fun Limo at the Wunderground Theatre, which is now a Coney Island. Wanting to improve his improv abilities he enrolled at University of Detroit Mercy and earned a Bachelor of Arts in Theatre and has been acting ever since. He performs on stage in the Detroit area and in films and commercials and appeared in a Collabfeature series that had a one season run on Amazon Prime entitled *A Billion to One*. While at UDM he took a creative writing course and discovered the wonderful expressive craft of poetry and the joy of writing fiction. He also holds a Master of Science in Marketing from Yeshiva University. Jacob is earning a Master of Fine Arts in Creative Writing from Concordia University - Saint Paul; after that onward and upwards as he hopes to be able to obtain his Ph.D in English. Jacob would like to thank his loving parents for their constant love, encouragement, and support; and he would like to thank you for reading.

Contact the author:
jplante81@gmail.com